**WHERE WE LIVE**

# WE LIVE IN A COUNTRY

by Jennifer Boothroyd

Consultant: Beth Gambro
Reading Specialist, Yorkville, Illinois

Minneapolis, Minnesota

# Teaching Tips

## Before Reading

- Look at the cover of the book. Discuss the picture and the title.
- Ask readers to brainstorm a list of what they already know about countries. What can they expect to see in the book?
- Go on a picture walk, looking through the pictures to discuss vocabulary and make predictions about the text.

## During Reading

- Read for purpose. Encourage readers to think about the country they live in as they are reading.
- Ask readers to look for the details of the book. What are they learning about the things people in a country share in common?
- If readers encounter an unknown word, ask them to look at the sounds in the word. Then, ask them to look at the rest of the page. Are there any clues to help them understand?

## After Reading

- Encourage readers to pick a buddy and reread the book together.
- Ask readers to name two things they might see in a country. Find the pages that tell about these things.
- Ask readers to write or draw something they learned about living in a country.

**Credits:**
Cover and title page, © hodim/Shutterstock; 3, © Rawpixel/iStock; 5, © PeopleImages/iStock, © Monkey Business Images/Shutterstock; 7, © FrankRamspott/iStock; 8–9, © mangostock/Adobe Stock; 11, © RomanR/Adobe Stock; 13, © Octavio Hoyos/Shutterstock; 14–15, © White House Photo/Alamy; 17, © Krakenimages.com/Shutterstock; 18–19, © xavierarnau/iStock; 20–21, © FatCamera/iStock; 22T, © Asatur Yesayants/Shutterstock; 22M, © artfoto53/Shutterstock; 22B, © heckepics/iStock; 23TL, © kali9/iStock; 23TR, © SeventyFour/iStock; 23BL, © LightField Studios/Shutterstock; 23BM, © anekoho/Adobe Stock; 23BR, © Krakenimages.com/Shutterstock.

Library of Congress Cataloging-in-Publication Data is available at www.loc.gov or upon request from the publisher.

ISBN: 979-8-88822-062-7 (hardcover)
ISBN: 979-8-88822-259-1 (paperback)
ISBN: 979-8-88822-377-2 (ebook)

Copyright © 2024 Bearport Publishing Company. All rights reserved. No part of this publication may be reproduced in whole or in part, stored in any retrieval system, or transmitted in any form or by any means, electronic, mechanical, photocopying, recording, or otherwise, without written permission from the publisher.

For more information, write to Bearport Publishing, 5357 Penn Avenue South, Minneapolis, MN 55419.

# Contents

**Faraway Friends** . . . . . . . . . . . . . . . . 4

Country Facts . . . . . . . . . . . . . . . . . . . . . . . . . . 22

Glossary . . . . . . . . . . . . . . . . . . . . . . . . . . . . . . . . 23

Index . . . . . . . . . . . . . . . . . . . . . . . . . . . . . . . . . . . . 24

Read More . . . . . . . . . . . . . . . . . . . . . . . . . . . . . 24

Learn More Online . . . . . . . . . . . . . . . . . . . . 24

About the Author . . . . . . . . . . . . . . . . . . . . . 24

# Faraway Friends

Today, we get to say hi to our friends.

We wave at them on a screen.

Their school is very far away.

It is in another country.

The land on Earth is divided up.

Each area is a different country.

There are almost 200 of them.

They are different shapes and sizes.

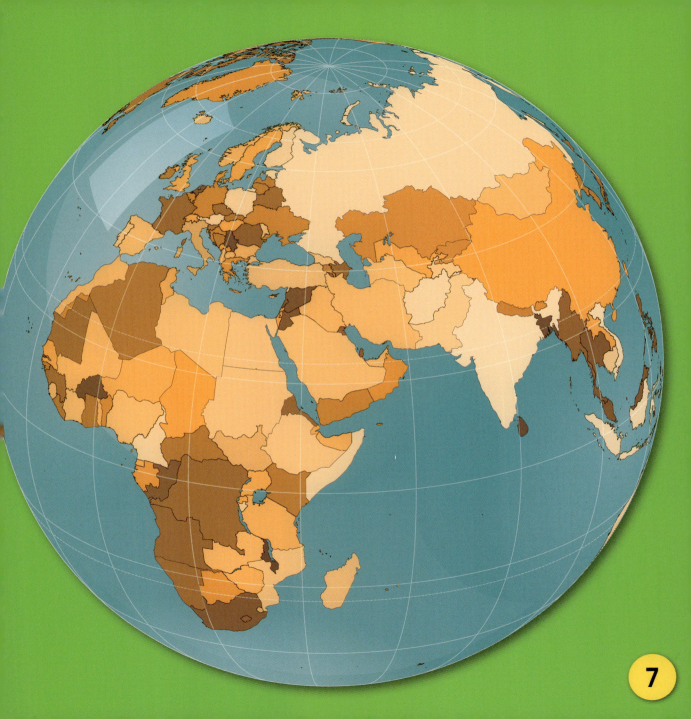
7

Each country has many people.

**Citizens** are people who are from a country.

Millions of citizens live in our country.

All the people in a country use the same money.

Most speak the same **language**.

Each country has a **government**.

The government helps its citizens stay well.

It makes rules called laws.

Some governments are led by one person.

Other places have a group.

The people in charge work together to run the country.

Citizens in many countries choose their leaders.

They do it by **voting**.

This lets people say what they want for their country.

What can people do for their country?

Learn about its past.

**Celebrate** its holidays.

These are the things that make a country special.

Our country has a lot of people.

We can all help make it great.

We love our country!

# Country Facts

The Olympics happen every two years. People from different countries get together to play sports.

Every country has a flag. The color red is on a lot of flags. Many flags have stars.

China and India are the countries with the most people.

22

# Glossary

**celebrate** to come together and enjoy a special event

**citizens** people who are from a country

**government** the people and bodies who lead a place

**language** the words that people speak or write

**voting** picking what you would like to happen

# Index

**citizens** 8, 12, 16
**government** 12, 14
**language** 10
**laws** 12

**money** 10
**sizes** 6
**voting** 16

# Read More

**Gaertner, Meg.** *My Country (Where I Live).* Lake Elmo, MN: Focus Readers, 2021.

**Rodriguez, Alicia.** *Country (Where Do I Live?).* New York: Crabtree Publishing Company, 2022.

# Learn More Online

1. Go to **www.factsurfer.com** or scan the QR code below.
2. Enter "**In a Country**" into the search box.
3. Click on the cover of this book to see a list of websites.

# About the Author

Jenny Boothroyd lives in the United States. She can drive to Canada in three hours. Someday, she would love to visit Japan and Italy.